**Plantation Souls** by Dr. Marlene Miles

Freshwater Press, USA

ISBN: 978-1-960150-25-7

Paperback Version

# Plantation Souls

## Dr. Marlene Miles

Freshwater

Freshwater Press

# Table of Contents

Welcome ....................................................5

NOTHING *NEVER* HAPPENS................................6

Vegas .......................................................7

Can You Hear It? .........................................9

Letting Things In.........................................12

Fire .........................................................13

The Secret .................................................18

Plantation America ......................................27

It Was War .................................................30

SOMETHING HAPPENED ..................................34

Something Happened .....................................35

Plantation Mentality .....................................41

Like Animals ...............................................45

Plantation Sex .............................................49

Can't Wait to be King ....................................53

THE KING'S DELICACIES..................................57

The King's Delicacies .....................................58

Survival.....................................................67

A Whole Person ...........................................70

Keep It......................................................76

DNA..........................................................78

Pick Your Side..............................................81

ONE SOUL ..................................................84

One Soul..................................................................85

The Boss..................................................................88

Love Yourself..........................................................95

Do The Work ...........................................................98

The Blood Is Crying Out .................................101

Do You Hear the Blood?...................................105

Do We Heal? ......................................................107

Benediction........................................................112

Other books by this author...........................113

# Welcome

Welcome to Black History Month, where I discuss the spiritual history of people who were stolen from Africa and were forced to come here to *Plantation America,* and what may have happened to them here.

*Happened*? well, what got in there may not be past tense, because if it got in the bloodline, it's not just history, it still might be happening.

Even today.

# NOTHING *NEVER* HAPPENS

# Vegas

Of course, I'm starting a book entitled, **Plantation Souls** talking about Las Vegas. Let the foolish things confound the wise.

We've all heard the campaign that what happens in Vegas stays in Vegas. Well, it doesn't, because while you're in Vegas, what happens to you in Vegas gets *into* you. What happens around you, what you participate in happens *to* you. If it can't get *in*, stuff will follow you home, hoping for a chance to get *in* or at least to influence you to sin, *again*.

Even if you don't participate in something, if you **see it,** sometimes if you only *hear* about it, it can affect you because faith comes by hearing. But especially if you participate in the thing, no matter how much fun you're having or think you're having, in the process of it all, you are being *changed*. It doesn't have to be a horror or a trauma to change you; "fun" changes people too.

So whatever happened in whatever big city or small town you were in, while either living there, vacationing there or just traveling through, you can bring it home with you, on you, or maybe even *in* you especially if you are not spiritually aware prepared and prayed up. Whatever happens in Vegas has really happened more *to* you and *in* you more than Vegas. As imperceptible as it may have been, you are being changed. We all are. Therefore, unless you stay in Vegas, whatever happened to you or whatever you did there is coming home with you. Once associated with you or attached to you, it's going wherever you're going.

Vegas was changed too, but very little compared to the change in *you*. Even if you lost all your money, stayed drunk and overate, Vegas was changed very little while you were changed a lot.

Even if you **stayed** in Vegas, you are still changed.

# Can You Hear It?

*Can a man take fire in his bosom and his clothes not be burned? Can one go upon hot coals and his feet not be burned?* Proverbs 6:27-28

Can a man take fire to his bosom and not be burned? We may not smell fire on you, but if you were in the fire, unless God *sent* you to the fire, you will get burned some kind of way. If you just sent yourself, if you decided, *"I'm going to Vegas because I want to go there,"* and you got caught up in some shenanigans in Vegas, something will happen to you, and you *will* be changed.

If God *sent* you with the promise that He would bring you through, there is nothing at all to worry about.

Can a man take fire and not be burned? I answer that with some other age-old questions, such as, *If a tree falls in the forest and there's no one to hear it, will it make a sound?* I say it will make a sound because it's a **law**. Whether spiritual or natural, or both, it's a law.

If the sun shines tomorrow morning but you don't choose to open your eyes, but instead you decide to sleep all day, the sun will still shine. If you're in Vegas, for example, and you stay awake all night, sleep all the next day, the sun is still coming up, and the sun will still shine even if _you_ don't look at it. Sun, shining is a law.

How do you know that someone else didn't hear the tree and someone else wanted and needed to hear that tree fall? Perhaps to step out of harm's way. If not a person, the forest animals?

We live in a world where God is the center of the Universe, not we ourselves.

God has set things in order.

In Genesis, God says that the blood of Abel is crying out from the ground. Can any one of us hear it? Abel's blood was crying out from the ground because he had been murdered. Could anyone of his generation hear it? God could. It was still making noise, even though no one was hearing it, but God. Some things are set in order. Blood will cry out from the ground; it's a spiritual law.

God also heard that tree fall. That tree had a purpose in the earth, shade, protection, a perch for His birds, a home for squirrels, ants; there are animals and living things depending on that tree.

God needed to hear that tree fall. God needed to know that the tree gave up, collapsed, or was murdered with a power saw or a bulldozer. God has animals that He is watching over and providing for.

His eye is on the sparrow, how much more is He watching over you?

If there's a flood on your street, for example, and the water levels rise up to your front door, will the water come in even if you're not looking at it? Of course, it will. Nature obeys the Laws of God. We should not only take notice of that, but man should also obey the Laws of God.

None of us are impervious to our environment, naturally speaking, but especially spiritually speaking. If we let stuff in, if we invite stuff in, it will come in. If your seal by the Holy Ghost isn't good enough, by no fault of the Holy Spirit, but by your own doing, if you're just willfully committing sins, *stuff* will come in. If that is the case you will bring it home from Vegas, any big city, any small town, or from life. Period.

# Letting Things In

Sometimes unexpected and undesirable things come in when there's a violation of the law. When speaking of letting things in, I'm talking about while living your everyday, regular life, not doing anything bizarre, like seeking weird meditations or the like. In our regular everyday life stuff can get in like water rising and rising, especially if you choose to wade in that water, get in that water, swim in that water, stoop down in the water. You might sink in that water. Or worse.

If we are really wise in our own conceits, we think we can outsmart everyone. The danger here is that is where most people get caught up and deceived into letting some stuff *in*. Some of this *stuff* can burn, so now we are playing with fire.

# Fire

Maybe you didn't know you were playing with fire, but isn't fire the thing that we always want to play with anyway? We want fire because it's *exciting*. We want fire because something inside us tells us or suggests to us that we want it. We want fire, we want the hot, but we don't want the burn. It's like you want a habanero or ghost pepper--, we want to see how hot we can take it without being burned.

We want the picante without the caliente. So how hot can we make it? How hot can we take it? We want the heat without the scorch. We want the heat without the singe. We want the hot without the stench of smoke on us after having played with that fire.

Playing dangerously with danger, we want see how much heat we can take before it hurts, while believing that it won't consume us. It's a foolish game. We certainly don't want the fire to follow us home. We want it to sit like it's a well-trained pet that we could just say, "*Heel*," or, "*Stay*," to and it'll stay where we leave it. We don't want that fire to follow us everywhere because there are certain people that we don't want to know that we've been playing with fire. Our parents, especially Mom, our spouse, Pastor? The boss at work.

However, we kind of want certain others to *know* that we've been playing with fire, because we want them to think that we're just that bad. We're bad like that; we might even embellish the fire story of the adventures in Vegas.

We really don't want everyone or *certain* ones to know we've been playing with fire. Too bad, really because the smell of smoke will be on anyone who plays with fire like that.

If we could tell FIRE to go to where we work and wait for us there so we can brag to our co-workers tomorrow morning, that would satisfy a lot of people. If we could leave it at the basketball court so we can show off to our bruh's how tough we really are, we'd do it. Some corrupt sons might brag to their corrupt dads about that fire in Vegas.

But we don't want that fire or the smell of its smoke to go home because if the wife finds out, there'll be trouble. We will have to do everything we can to keep the spouse from finding out about this fire play.

Women might want to leave that fire in the trunk of the car with those three new pairs of shoes that she plans to sneak into the house. This fire can be shared with her girlfriends, but hubby will definitely not like knowing she did this.

If you could see fire, it's like a clingy friend who you've spent time with and as much as you try to hide, it will follow you because **FIRE** wants everyone to know that **you've** been playing with *it*. If Fire had a Facebook page, it would post a picture of **you** on it.

Let me say now: sin is fire. For those in the back, *sin is fire*. For those in the nosebleed section: SIN IS FIRE. For those in the overflow room: Sin is fire. For those barely listening, sin is fire. And you who didn't bring your glasses to read this book: SIN IS FIRE.

Now that you've sinned, *you're different,* whether you're in Vegas or some small town, you're different. Yeah, you know how your kids look different from day-to-day, especially young kids, because they're always growing and changing. Well, so do you. So do we all, and I'm not talking about your size.

We look *spiritually* different every day. We either look good, because we did things spiritually correct, or to our detriment, we might look bad if we decided to play with fire yesterday or last night. We look different based on what we've chosen to do or to not do. What we've allowed to happen to us by default or what we've been around, what we've experienced or participated in or worse, *invited* to happen to us. So listen, even if we haven't allowed anything negative to happen to us, we might look different because we've been in the Spirit. Hallelujah. We've been praying. We may have been fasting, or up all night. We may have gotten up to take the 3rd or the 4th Watch as God woke you up to do just that. So we may look fantastic today. And because we didn't sin, God may have renewed our strength.

Or we might look terrible because something happened. Because nothing *never* happens. Something always happens. So whether we realize it fully or not, things *changed*. Whether we participated or not, things changed, something happened. Something always happens. So, when somebody says where have you been? You really can't say nowhere. Who were you with? Nobody. No, that's not really true, is it? What happened? Nothing? No, that's impossible, because nothing **_never_** happens.

# The Secret

Something did happen. But you're not telling it, huh? Your friends aren't telling. Doesn't matter, because what happened in Vegas or whatever big city or little town you were in, it will tell on you, even if you think you're keeping it a secret.

Your secret will tell on you. Your secret makes you behave differently, especially if you have a conscience. If you repent, your secret will only have the power to make you behave differently, temporarily. But if you don't repent, that sin, that sin nature gets into you, and will change you permanently because if you act differently long enough, you will *become* different, your behavior will be different, and it may even change you permanently.

Even if you don't have a conscience, the secret might change you. It may change you from having a conscience to not having a conscience, because now you believe or you're trying to believe you're the greatest actor in the world and no one can see through your act. When you should really be feeling remorse or guilt or something, you may be feeling nothing. So you *act* the same. Now you have a seared conscience.

(No, I'm not saying that actors have a seared conscience. Actors are portraying roles, hopefully they're not hiding a real crime, sin, or some other nefarious activity.)

But your secret can tell on you by the way you talk about it constantly, or absolutely refuse to talk about it. Your secret can tell on you by the way *you* act, by the way you pretend, the way you gaslight, saying the exact opposite of what really happened. Your secret may tell on you by the way you project, saying somebody else did something when you're the someone who did the something.

Your secret may tell on you by the way you voluntarily offer information about it when no one asked. You're the one who keeps bringing it up. There are a myriad of other telltale signs that *something happened*, and if you keep talking or not talking about it, you will end up telling what happened, when, to whom, and *with* whom.

Your behavior, whether you are trying to conceal something or not will tell on you. It will be told to the discerning eye and also to the simply observant. It can't be hidden. The sin that you did or the sin that *happened* to you, even if it was forced, will be crying out. People who know of it may not be trying to find out why you're the way you are, or why you're different. The sin just cries out, like the blood, or the tree that falls in the forest, and you may not have even known that you can hear it, but somehow you do.

Somehow someone hears and not to condemn you, it's because of the Love that God has for us all, and even for trees.

It's so the hearer can help. It's so he that needs help can be helped. If sin had a Facebook page it would post your picture right on it. Sin is proud. Sin is proud to know you, proud it got with **you**, even when we are not proud of sin, it is proud of us in a sick, sick way. Man, mankind is a real catch; sin is proud to affiliate with you and will tell it every time in subtle or loud ways.

The new and different things you now **know** are telling on you. The Tree of the KNOWLEDGE of Good & Evil is still working. New knowledge, good or bad, godly, or evil makes you *different*. It did for both Adam & Eve.

That knowledge, that sin made them quiet. Sneaky.

When your kids are too quiet, you go immediately to see what they are up to or into. I think Adam & Eve got quiet and God didn't like the sound of that silence. Or, like the tree in the forest that *fell,* God heard it, but not the two who were standing right beside it. God talks to nature; would it not stand to reason that nature also talks to God? We don't know that the tree didn't scream out to God when the fruit was forced from its limbs.

In sin, you may think if you get quiet and secretive, you can get away, but sin cannot be hidden. Got new tricks? Do you have a new hairdo, new outfits? All these things are telling on you, and you really can't hide what you *think* you're hiding.

I didn't say it was dark in Vegas, but what's done in the dark, no matter how many friends or how many other people *approved* it, no matter if you all voted on it, no matter how many people made a pact to never tell, it'll come to light, it will be found out, and that's for real.

So, the secret is because of the thing that you did, or it's the thing that was done to you, or the thing that happened around you that you just saw, even if you were an innocent bystander. I'm serious. Imagine you saw a car accident. You're not even in the accident, but it affects you. You may be in shock, or awe, or amazement, or fear. The experience has changed you.

*Nothing* **never** happens. Something is happening all day, every day, spiritually speaking.

The soldier that goes off to war may be in the action, he may be seeing action, he may not be, but he may come back from deployment changed. He may be suffering with PTSD because something happened in him, even if nothing happened directly to him. He was in a war or warlike environment.

Maybe something happened to a buddy. Or maybe he saw something, even just a building, get blown up. We have seen over and again what happened on 9/11 that's affected all of us. *Nothing* **never** happens.

Some things that we see happen change us, and some things are so subtle, culture, tradition, simple words spoken, good or bad that change us.

Daily. They change us. Maybe you watched a racy TV show or movie back in your own living room, and now you see the opposite gender in a certain negative light. But you don't really know that you see them differently—yet. Over time, the manifestation of what got in you will show. It may take you until you're 30 years old to realize the way you're treating women is because you *changed* when you watched an R-rated film when you were 13 years old. It may take you until you're 35 to realize why you feel that all men are dogs, because you listened to a raunchy standup when you were 16 and it really colored your life; it ruined your life really because you have treated men a certain negative way for the entire time that most are dating, marrying and starting to have kids. While there you were hating men whom you'd never met.

You must guard your eyes, your ears, guard your heart, because something is happening all the time. The environment we live in and grow in affects us negatively or positively, in ungodly or Godly ways 24/7. This spiritual warfare may not be bullets or rockets flying, it could be *words*. It could be visual impacts. It could be food that should not be eaten. It could be food that should be left uneaten, for example when a person is on a fast, that lasagna is part of a warfare to make you fail in the fast. Vegas has buffets and fantastic chefs, btw. Food and drinks are many times the first enticement to sin. Just saying.

*Nothing* **never** happens. Impacts are made on you, on us every day, maybe all day. We're in spiritual warfare all day long, whether we realize it or not. That's why we keep our minds on Jesus. By warfare I mean that things are bombarding us all day long; some of us realize it and have on the armor of God, some think there is nothing happening because they cannot see or hear it.

If you could hear the din of the devil's warfare around you, would you believe it? No. There are people who *can* hear in the Spirit and most people think they, themselves are crazy because they haven't met anyone who can tell them what they are hearing, and without God they don't have a clue.

There are others who don't have God, didn't have God and they've been captured, deceived, and working for the devil now. If their seeing gifts are not fully grounded in God, they may be getting false inputs from *familiar spirits*; the devil is a confirmed counterfeiter.

There are people who can SEE in the Spirit and people also think they are crazy because humans don't seem to think knowing anything about the spirit has a purpose or validity even though we are all *spirit*. Seers can be considered crazy too. Be assured, the seers and the hearers in the Spirit may have those gifts to tell you and others, things that could help their lives or even save their lives. However, if the hearers and seers have not been nurtured in the things of God, they do seem as if they are rambling on.

By seers and hearers, I am speaking of people with bona fide Godly prophetic mantles, not psychics who get their information from demons, *familiar spirits, guardian demons, spirit guides* and fallen angels from the second heaven. Remember, the devil is spiritual so a spiritual "feeling" could accompany false, demonic information – a surge, a sense of power, but if it is not of God, it is a lie that is designed to steal, kill and destroy you and any others that the warfare is aimed against. **Demonic recoil from flesh weapons will get you, even if you think you have a mighty weapon trained on someone you hate.**

We're to stay prayerful. We're to watch and pray. We're to praise and worship. We're to stay in the Word and keep the Word in us. We're supposed to wear the whole armor of God, because there is spiritual warfare all day, every day. It has been this way since Adam & Eve who in disobedience became victims and casualties of that warfare (war).

**Nothing** *never* **happens**. God is telling us that we need protection from spiritual things while we're in the natural, because we are *spirit*, we are *spirits*. He tells us how to do it, and God even provides all the PPE, that is the spiritual armor.

Put it on. It's not optional. Put it on. Things are happening every day. Even Disney's Cinderella knows that things are happening every day and she's a cartoon.

# Plantation America

So, you grew up in a family that influenced and shaped who you are. You get married; marriage may shape or reshape who you are. Imagine if you were carried away into captivity or born into captivity, having to do everything that you're told to do. That would certainly shape who you are and who you would become as it gets *in you* and impacts you. The effects of what affects you is soon seen.

Imagine if you were born as a slave in Plantation America. It's Black History Month, so I'm talking about, writing about how slavery **forced** changes in people. It forced changes even in the culture and in the land. It forced changes in people's behavior every day on, around, near or regarding Plantation America.

The Plantation led to serious *spiritual* changes in people. It led to sin and more sin. Sin fires raged as Colonists behaved as if there was no longer a God in Heaven, a Bible to follow or even common decency and manners. Even if everyone in the Colonies voted for slavery, did God? Some opted to accept, invite or to go get demonic curses for themselves and their families by chasing money and behaving horrendously in Plantation America.

For others, the Plantation **forced** curses on them. Word curses were being spoken over people. They were degraded and spoken to harshly.

Lineages, names, identities were stolen, lost, taken away, or discarded--, however you want to look at it. This would result in identity crises.

There was blatant robbery. The entire value of people's life and work was **stolen**; they were not even allowed their own wages.

Yeah, nothing *never* happens. You can't say because slavery is over that nothing happened or that people should *get over it*.

Wait! Slavery is not over. There are approximately 50 million slaves in the Earth, in the natural right now, or didn't you know? Last year five states voted to allow slavery which they are calling indentured servitude (again) as punishments for crime, in the USA. It passed in four states; Alabama, Tennessee, Vermont and Oregon. US citizens, are you paying attention???

Back to Plantation America: Things happened. Family life was at risk daily. You didn't know if somebody was going to take your wife or your life. You didn't know if your husband would come home from the blazing fields, or if your kids would be gone and never seen again, sold, or something worse. Slaves have not had and, have no protection from anything really, even heinous things, including murder.

A slave didn't have security in whether they, or anyone else in their family would see tomorrow.

There was forced sexual sin by violence, that's what makes it *forced*. Slave masters appear to be unregistered sex offenders and perverts. (Today, most slaves, 45 million of them are in forced labor, leaving approximately 5 million or more as sex slaves worldwide.)

# It Was War

Short-term violence is a battle, but sustained violence is war. Plantation America was **WAR**. It was a one-sided war declared on some people from Africa who had no real weapons and didn't know war was coming **except the Lord may have told them**. We will go deeper into this later.

Enslaved people are never brought willingly to any destination. These were no different; they were chained and dragged into this country or any of the other countries they were dropped off at, I mean sold to, (Brazil and the Caribbean.)

*Things* happened to these enslaved people in this hemisphere, more things than had already happened in their countries of origin. They may have been captured in battles and village raids in Africa. Sold on an auction block there to Portuguese, Spanish, Brazilian, German, and Dutch slave traders. Those who endured the Middle Passage, only to be put on another auction block and sold again in North America--, Plantation America.

On this American Plantation, they may have been forced to agree with word curses over them or be beaten, again, or even killed. They may have been required to renounce the *God* they were serving. Depends on if they love their life more than they loved God. No one but God can know what a person will do in slavery, survival, or war-like situations.

Africans were suddenly forced into a culture they may have never known. Forced labor, captivity --all the stuff that happened on and around the plantation in Plantation America got ***in there*** and African slaves were changed. It takes approximately 3 generations for things to ***get in there***. Plantation America lasted 250 years. Jim Crow lasted another 100 years for those who believe it's over. Three hundred-fifty-plus years is more than enough time for **permanent** changes to happen in people, in families, down bloodlines.

After going through the Plantation America "war" that led up to the Civil War that led to Jim Crow, folks have the nerve to ask, Why are *they* like that? Well, why do you think *they* are like that? It's because **something happened to them**.

Something happened because nothing *never* happens and what got in there was forced in there and I suppose it has to be forced out.

Something spiritual happened and you can't just yell, *"Cut!"* like it's the end of a movie scene. You can't just say *"Never mind,"* or just tell people to get over it. It's not like it's over and it's a movie or play and everybody goes back to normal, whatever that was. Their regular life wasn't here, in this country, in Brazil or in the Caribbean in forced labor and/or sexual service. So, after Emancipation, what were they supposed to *go back to?*

Plantation America was a secret war in plain sight. Colonists were brutal; as soon as they got here, they waged war against Native Americans, Plantation America, the Revolutionary War and the Civil War, Jim Crow… all these wars were on *this soil.*

Oh, don't take it personally, the Chinese were exploited from 1863-1869 to build the Transcontinental Railroad. In 1942 127,000 Japanese were put in internment camps forcing them to abandon property and businesses. Don't say anything to me about Hispanics being separated from their families and put in cages at the border starting in 2017. IMPRISONMENT and slavery affect people spiritually, negatively. It damages their souls, sometimes it murders their souls.

You should believe in forgiveness but know what you're forgiving. After being set free on paper, ALWAYS do the spiritual work and get deliverance and restoration for your soul to get the stench of that fire and the smoke off of you.

**He restoreth my soul**: he leadeth me in the paths of righteousness for his name's sake, (Psalm 23:3)

# SOMETHING
# HAPPENED

# Something Happened

Something happened. The scene is Plantation America where a lot of things have happened to a lot of people.

What happened on the Plantation obviously didn't **stay** on the Plantation, like what's supposed to stay in Vegas just because you want it to stay in Vegas. I suppose a lot of people may have wanted a lot of things to stay on the Plantation, but it didn't. It couldn't.

It was impossible to stay there because what happened got *into* people and people migrate, they move around. They have children who move and migrate from place to place, town to town, city to city. Plantation stuff got in to people and it changed them. Then they had kids that came here a certain way, but that way was shaped by the home they grew up in, so in a real sense even though we think there are no more slave plantations in America, the Plantation is still happening. It is still happening unless every single and solitary soul has been delivered from every effect of Plantation America. It is still happening because it happened *to* people and got **IN** people.

It happened to souls, turning them into Plantation Souls. Then the *spirit* of the thing keeps happening once it's allowed or permitted to happen, because the *spirit* lasts forever. You also can't just do something once to get it out of your system, because doing it, even once, is what gets it *into* your system. Therefore, until you stop it, it doesn't stop. Sometimes it doesn't stop until you resist it. Still, sometimes it just doesn't stop.

For example, the well-meaning parent who tells his child, *"Don't go out there messing with those white women, they will kill you for that."*

Or the well-meaning parent who says to his child, *"Don't go out there messing with them Blacks, they steal you know, and they want to rape our women."*

Plan-tation.

We all need God.

Plantation America happened in souls, and it happened for 250 years and 100 more years of Jim Crow. That's 12 generations. So that's four times the number of generations it takes for a stronghold to take hold in a person, in a family, in a bloodline.

Of course, I'm speaking of negative changes--, curses, because no one would reject or complain about a blessing. Sometimes people have been forced *or tricked* into agreeing with curses over their own lives.

Anytime you hear or it is implied, *"Repeat after me,"* consider strongly what you are hearing and what you are asked to or possibly forced to repeat.

In Plantation America, every foul word spoken over every soul was a word curse. The oppressor probably believed every foul word to be true because he/she was indoctrinated already. *"These savages, these beasts, these n\*ggers are less than human."*

Slaves who didn't know English, suffered. And by their inability to defend themselves, by their forced silence, they suffered more, and were basically agreeing with those word curses.

The actions and the words of those things spoken were all **curses**. I can't think of any slave story where a slave was *blessed* on a plantation.

Blessings or cursings? If there are no blessings, then what? Cursings.

A curse gets in a person, and then in that family, and then continues down their bloodline. The person who curses a man saying that he is dumb or stupid or will never be successful in business is pronouncing a *perpetual* curse. First to that man, then down his family line, except that man or someone in his family realizes that a real curse has been spoken into him and his bloodline, and he has the knowledge and ability to break it. If he does not, it may devastate his entire bloodline for generations to come. A curse is no light matter, ***unopposed.***

We have no idea how many curses were spoken over how many slaves, and those curses got into their bloodlines until we **see** the failures down their bloodlines and backtrack to put it all together, then BREAK those curses.

What got into the enslaved, was forced in there and I suppose it has to be forced out of there.

The Plantation was 400 years ago, you might argue. Yeah, but the Plantation ***changed*** people, and I'd say it changed most people for the worse. These changes are real. Curses can continue up to 14 generations and longer if they keep getting renewed, unknowingly down a bloodline. Reiterating, by the time any change, any something, any--, *thing*, gets into a **bloodline**, into a family line, by the third generation is *in there*. It's now considered generational. It's a stronghold.

It doesn't mean that it will always be there because deliverance is still possible. But it will take a strong deliverance when it's in there deep, generationally like that. It will take a strong dedication to the Word and to resisting sin, and it will take a godly lifestyle to fight generational curses from lingering or reentering. Therefore, submit yourself to God, resist the devil, and he will flee from you, (James 4:7).

Apostle Paul said this to the Romans:

I do not understand what I do. For what I want to do I do not do. But what I hate, I do. And if I do what I do not want to do, I agree that the law is good as it is. It is no longer I myself who do it, but it is sin living in me. But I know that good itself does not dwell in me. That is in my sinful nature, where I have the desire to do what is good but I cannot carry it out. Or I do not do the good I want to do, but the evil I do not want to do. This I keep on doing. Now if I do what I do not want to do, it is no longer I who do it, but it is sin living in me that does it. (Romans 7:15-20)

That is a stronghold. Once sin gets *in*, by the third generation, it's a stronghold. A generation is about 20 to 30 years--, 250 years, how long slavery was "legal" in the States is about 8 generations.

God is visiting to the $3^{rd}$ and $4^{th}$ generations for a reason. It is the test to see if a bloodline PASSED or failed based on what's in the Third Generation's visit. God is gracious to give a bloodline more than 100 years to take an OPEN BOOK test. Open the Book, people and pass the spiritual tests of your bloodline so you can be pleasing to God and get blessed.

That which I would do. I don't do that. That which I don't want to do, that's what I find myself doing. This is serious spiritual interference. Deliverance is needed. So, what got *in there* was forced in there in Plantation America. So, it has to be forced out of there. Forced out by Truth. Forced out by *deliverance*.

# Plantation Mentality

Plantation Mentality is:

- **Taking care of other people's stuff and leaving your own work undone.**
- **Taking care of *certain* people's stuff and leaving other people's stuff undone** because maybe the *other* people aren't as important or don't deserve the respect as *certain* people do. That is a plantation mentality.
- **Not taking care of your own stuff** is a plantation mentality where a person may have been beat down to the point where they don't think they're worthy of being treated well, honoring themselves, or being treated decently, or having nice things.

You should honor yourself. We should love ourselves, not obsessively but respectfully, moderately, all things in balance. Because we are fearfully and wonderfully made, we honor God by honoring and taking care of His creation, and that includes ourselves.

We are also to respect others, no matter where they come from, no matter what they look like, and no matter how much money they appear to have, or not have.

Another Plantation Mentality is:

- **Expecting people to do things for you: entitlement.**

Do your own work instead. I know a fellow who must believe he had a previous life, and he may believe he was a king in that previous life. I'm not sure of what size kingdom he thought he had, but he really thinks everyone should be his servant. No, that's not where we are. Not anymore.

Another Plantation Mentality is:

- **Admiring other races more than your own**. No. Just as people are taught to love themselves, they can also be taught, trained, and forced to *hate themselves.*

This is really a war; look at the propaganda. Taking care of other people and not yourself. The Bible says to love your neighbor as yourself, not *instead* of yourself. I could go on about this, maybe another book, but not this one. Here's where you can pick a side:

- Thinking your race is superior to another or others is yet another Plantation mentality.

Just as the mascot or the cheerleaders pump up the crowd at football game, it's a rally. The purpose of the rally is to convince you that this is the best team, the coach is the best coach, the players are the best, and even the fans are the best. It's a rally. People are trained to believe they're superior, and that is an issue that makes me wonder if someone is not feeling *inferior*.

To me, the word, *race* indicates that we all should be going somewhere and doing something with a quickness rather than standing around arguing, fighting, bickering, hurting each other. Just because there's no point on your pencil doesn't mean there shouldn't be one to your life. If you spend your whole life trying to beat another guy down, when do you do the will of God?

When will you do what God said for you to do instead of stealing, killing, and destroying people as the devil has instructed? Destroying another's self-image and breaking down their goals and their purpose and stealing their life's work and their life's income is stealing, killing, and destroying.

That is devil work. That is not God's work. Here's more devil work: For trying to learn how to read, slaves got their thumbs cut off. They were mangled. Some of them had toes cut off, for trying to run away. As a slave you'd have to be beat down pretty good to *not* want to run away. That would mean that Plantation mentality had gotten down into your soul. That's when you know that you are really captive. That's when you know that you are REALLY a slave.

Today, if you are third (fourth, or more) generation from slavery and you are complacent, beat down, hopeless, apathetic... these are clues that you are still on the Plantation.

If you are third or fourth generation and you still think you are better than "those people," you feel you are entitled and that everything belongs to you, then you and your bloodline are also still on the Plantation.

Plantation America was a war, and it persists. Remnants of it today are in the generations. There are still people who mock others for pursuing an education. Some people think you don't need to get educated. There are people who are jealous of other people who are educated. Some try to tear others down, some try to steal the credentials and the work, the labor of others.

# Like Animals

Yet another plantation mentality:

- Treating people like animals, like cattle (chattel). Families were broken up with no sense of conscience in Plantation America.

The residual of that today is that families are too easily broken up if they ever even come together as a family. Have people really forgotten how to have a family? How to be in a family? Or has that been beaten out of people during this 400+ years of Plantation mentality?

There's more. There's the part where the captor tried to make you believe that you were an animal so he could treat you like one--, less than a human. Surely don't embrace that part. Or the part where you were degraded daily and taught to degrade others who looked like you; surely don't embrace that part.

Surely you must resist the part where the oppressor tried to murder your soul, and then threaten to or even killed the body. There were beatings and murders and lynchings straight out of the devil's handbook. Please, nobody embrace that part, and certainly not the part where the oppressor tried to murder your soul and then *deputize* you to also murder the souls of others, telling you that that was OK. No, we won't embrace that part.

Beloved, I pray that you will fight for your own soul and that you will not choose to or try to murder the soul of another just because the oppressor did it to the people in your family line. *Soul murder* got *in there*, it got into souls, into families, into households, and bloodlines.

An oppressive *spirit* that drives you to do that which you would not do, instead of doing what you really want to do is the net result of evil being accepted, embraced, or forced into you and your bloodline. This was done in Plantation America because something--, a lot of things *happened*.

No matter how passionately people deny the Plantation and the evils that happened on those Plantations, it happened because nothing *never* happens, and something did happen. All of this happened. All of these things happened. Evil and wrong and ignorance and stupidity and arrogance got into people-- **on both sides.**

Yes, I said that.

Unless spiritual and soul work is done to rid oneself of Plantation Mentality, it's still in there. It's still in bloodlines, and it's in family lines.

The work to be done to get it out of there is accepting Jesus Christ as your Lord and Savior. That's the work: Receiving deliverance, receiving truth, resisting the devil, devilish behaviors, evil events, and resisting devilish people. Because nothing *never* happens, something always happens, and something definitely happened in Plantation America.

It's far past Juneteenth; all of us should have to come off the Plantation, come out of the Wilderness, walk into the Promised Land, into the Kingdom of God. The Kingdom is the only haven. That's why today we still see the residual of plantation life in some people groups.

People are still bonding loosely to one another, because of the generational fear of losing another prematurely, violently, suddenly, or permanently. People are really afraid to love.

There are still those who are incapable of love because generationally their spirits were broken. Their souls were damaged; they have broken hearts that span decades and generations in their families. Hope deferred makes the heart sick and believing the worst, expecting the worst, expecting instead of hoping, expecting instead of having faith--, losing all hope. Hopelessness is the result of the heart being made sick.

That's why *they* are like this: heart disease, high blood pressure, mind disease, unbelief, despair, depression, and desperation running rampant in those bloodlines.

Listening to a modern-day, brokenhearted mother whose stud-service husband ran the streets and left her is *straight up* Plantation. The child who hears this is not likely to run to get married. And if he or she does, the spiritual influences that carried over from the Plantation that are in their bloodline will fight a successful, godly marriage.

This is what having a Plantation Soul does to a life. It destroys it. Even now.

# Plantation Sex

Bad things happened to people on the Plantation. The enslaved person with no autonomy didn't have to choose sin. He learned to steal, to eat. He learned to kill and destroy because he was forced to. One cannot choose to be raped; else it is consent. He was forced into survival mode because that's what happens to humans in war.

Plantation America was war. If you say America was not at war then you probably also believe the devil does not exist.

The somethings that happened changed the people, all the people, the generations, and the bloodlines. The fires of Plantation America did this, and the smoke of it is still on people to this day. You can tell by their behavior. You can tell by how life is defeating them that they are still under curses.

While researching my own family tree some years ago, I saw an early 1800 census where one "farmer" had two slaves. There were two

African women of childbearing age. That's all the slaves that farm had. This man had no wife and no children, just two African women of child-bearing age. Wonder what kind of crops he was growing? We don't even need to guess what sexual slavery was, that it was real in Plantation America.

You know, what got into folks by forced sexual activity should not astound you, but it probably would. Sexual sin is a huge portal for demonic entrance and activity. Nothing *never* happens. Something *always* happens. While working under the guise that creating more slaves was a money-making proposition, people were forced into base human nature. It was in full swing and all the while the devil has open season to move demon *spirits* around and *into* folks at will. Really.

Plantation America created many demonic portals.

No slave was off limits to sexual harassment. There was no protection for slaves from sexual harassment, rape, or forced pregnancy. Stolen children were sold--, the Lord knows where.

The men were trained to perform stud service.

**Nothing. Never. Happens**.

How many men still think that *that* was fun? And that's the part they want to take from the Plantation and continue to do that like they have their pick of all and everybody, anyone, anytime? This is the result of 250 years of teaching that this is okay; it's not.

Deliverance is needed right now--, big time. So, what got in there was forced in there, and I suppose it's got to be forced out of there.

You should never be afraid of deliverance. Sometimes deliverance is just somebody telling you the truth and you're hearing it for the very first time and it changes you. It changes you because it gets into your heart, it gets into your spirit, and it changes your soul. It changes your life. Get some sound Bible teaching; there is deliverance in that.

The next Plantation Mentality is:

- **Rejecting your own children**.

Let somebody else take care of them. Children were taken away on the plantations and there was nothing any slave person could do about it.

Evil was always happening on plantations, and it was how we have come to see that the things that they were growing on the plantations as also evil. To me, if it was an evil plantation, what was growing on the plantation was cursed and also evil. Shouldn't we consider the source, the course, and the curse? A lot of what they were growing we find out now is not good for us anyway, such as tobacco and sugar.

What you learned in captivity, you do if you're *forced* to in captivity. You do it because you have to, or you believe that you have to. But when you get out of captivity, *what now?* Do you still yearn for leeks, garlic, and cucumbers? What you've learned in captivity, you should stop. Unless it's *in you*. You can't stop if it's in you already, if it's a stronghold already you need deliverance.

# Can't Wait to be King

Oh? If you're not fully delivered, maybe you just can't wait to be king yourself so you can do the same evil to others that's been done to you.

Is that what you learned? Is that all you've learned from this ordeal? It depends on the prosperity or lack of prosperity of one's soul as to how they handle all that happened to them (their bloodline) as a result of Plantation America. Does one wake up grieving the day thinking this is wrong, or does one celebrate the evil of each day? Depends on who you are, who your God is, if you're serving Him and what side you're on. Some people are evil; they love evil, and thrive on it.

Rejoicing in evil is not God's way.

Others still have a conscience and a heart for God.

I desire to do your will. My God, your law is
within my heart, (Psalm 40:8).

You've got to know God so you can deal with and stay alive on the Plantation. Slavery is not fair.

Learning from the Hebrews who were slaves and came out of Egypt, but wandered in the Wilderness, you've got to fight externally to survive that Wilderness.

**AND** you have to fight internally what's been put in you, either overtly, covertly, or what you may have accepted as a coping mechanism. In your family now, you've got to look at yourself and let the Spirit judge what's been put *in there* historically, even by well-meaning family members and parents who have told you, over the generations, how to navigate this not fair life that's been handed to you. The average person probably wants to just forget all about the Plantation. But it needs to be looked at forensically and dealt with.

The Word of God says *Do not desire the king's dainties. Do not desire the king's delicacies.* Do not desire to be like an evil king. Do not desire the "good" of slavery. Do not deceive yourself. There's no good in it. Do not desire the perceived *good* of captivity.

Do not desire the *good* of sin. The Plantation Master was in sin; he was in all evil. You don't want to be like him, or like that.

All of Plantation America was gaslighted and they convinced people that what was right was wrong and what was wrong was right, and that sin was okay, especially sexual sin because they were all into their lusts and perversions, and that is sin—**full force**.

When people learn to like the sin life, that's the part that they want to stay in Vegas, because they liked the heat, but if the secret gets out there will be a burn. Sadly, they are more concerned about another human finding out than that God already knows. Oh sinner man/woman, there will be more than one burn from that sin, the only one you might avoid is if another human doesn't find out about it.

An unprospered soul in Plantation America may celebrate the sexual sin if he felt he benefitted from it, if it is the stuff they really wanted to do because it became a stronghold and they learned to like the benefits of having done it, even though it was sin. It was the only *good thing* that they had out of a bad situation, so they've convinced themselves it was *good.*

It wasn't.

I'm describing everything you have heard on television in every spiritually bad contract, agreement and covenant that was ever made since the history of time. The old bait and switch which shows you something good but is really taking away so much more--, maybe *everything.*

What comes after is far worse and creates that stronghold.

Ask EVE, ask Adam what came along with that Apple. Just a spoonful of sugar helps that medicine go down. *Something* happened in Plantation America. A lot of *something's* happened and almost all of it was bad for a soul, for any soul on either side. Bad for the spirit, bad for humans, bad for individuals, bad for families. Bad for bloodlines.

We all need Jesus. We all need deliverance.

# THE KING'S DELICACIES

# The King's Delicacies

We remember the fish we ate in Egypt at no cost.
Also the cucumbers, melons, leeks, onions and garlic,
(Numbers 11:5 NIV).

The American plantation: I'm calling it Plantation America where millions were enslaved.

Slavery wasn't right. It wasn't fair. As we all know, the Israelites were in the Wilderness trying to make their way to the Promised Land. You've got to fight externally to survive a Wilderness, but you also have to fight internally so that what's been put in you in years, decades, even centuries of slavery and captivity and oppression, does not conquer or defeat you.

What's been put in your spirit, and soul--, by all those other competing *spirits* that desire that you do wrong instead of doing right and has been put in you either overtly, by force, or you've *allowed* things in to cope. What's been put in there historically by well-meaning family members, even how to navigate this, not-fair life that you've been placed or dragged into needs to be at least evaluated and at most *put out* of you!

You've got an external fight to survive! And you've got an internal fight to live! Which one is more difficult depends on what's *in there* and how tight the stronghold.

Once you are free *on paper*, you still have to get free in your mind. (The mind is part of your soul.)

Finally, you're free. Even if you feel that now you get to be king, don't give in to that temptation. Do not desire the king's delicacies, do not desire his dainties. Do not reach back for the "good" of slavery, or the good of captivity, or the good of sin. Because what's bad comes right along with whatever you think is good. And that describes every bait and switch contract that's ever happened in the history of time.

The devil is very tricky. So in talking about Plantation America, we are talking about slavery, where there were **forced** changes of behavior in people which led to **forced curses** in people.

Word curses were spoken over people as they were degraded and downgraded. Slaves were also forced into sexual sin, most often by violence.

Sexual sin is one of the surest routes for the devil to get demons into a life, and into a bloodline.

Violence can be a brief battle, but sustained violence is **war**. Hundreds of years of conflict and violence, that's a war. Anybody who talks about Plantation America, if they don't describe it as a war and an unfair war, is doing a disservice. They are misinformed or lying.

War was declared on this people group, and they were captured and sold from Africa. Did anybody do anything about it? Not really, because they were *sold*. So, it appears not. No one seemed to care. Maybe that was the worst of things or the best of things. I don't know—getting out of a pagan, idolatrous continent could have been a good thing. Being sold into captivity, hard labor and slavery of all kinds had to have been the worst thing.

The Colonists physically overpowered the captured Africans, but spiritually, what protection did Colonists have against the ***strong spirituality*** of African peoples? Oh, they didn't believe in it? **Whether or not you believe in something has no bearing on its existence.** Having no spiritual or inadequate spiritual protection is stupid, actually-

-, then and now, in Plantation America, or in *Vegas*.

Unopposed witchcraft is very powerful. If you don't believe that witchcraft exists, then you won't oppose it. Witchcraft was probably one of the biggest reasons why the Africans were allowed to be captured and brought here. I am convinced that they were in trouble with God because God is not cruel and white Colonists did not have Manifest Destiny as they claimed.

Coming to a lawless Plantation stripped of all the rights of a human being was absolutely the worst thing. Sold into captivity, robbed daily, beaten, whipped and brutalized, terrorized, raped, and murdered--, if God allowed this, they were in trouble with God. Big time.

They were put into unyielding servitude, having their life's blood essentially drained from them and their life's wages stolen from them.

If somebody didn't give you a paycheck for one day or one week, you would raise Cain.

At the beginning, during, and at the end of a slave's life, he had nothing. This is all of their entire life. 40 years, 50 years. I don't know how long they were even *allowed* to live or how the conditions were. If you just work all the time, there's no downtime, there's no vacation. Then all their money that they would have earned is **stolen**.

They're sweating and toiling in the fields as the plantation owner is pocketing all the revenue and exalting himself as a little g *god*? That's at the most, but in the least he exalted himself as a king.

An enslaved people were forced to agree with word curses over themselves, or maybe continue to be beaten, or worse, killed. It appears that most of their lives they feared death. So maybe they gave in to these demonic requests and requirements of the Plantation. Maybe they had to swear oaths to the Plantation *kings* and the plantation *gods*, those demonic *gods* that rule these Plantations. You won't convince me that they weren't there, because they were.

They were there to dominate slaves and to degrade them to the point of cursing themselves, so the plantation *kings* could have dominion and control. This is all demonic.

The Plantation *kings* declared war on people and took them captive, where those people had not accosted these Plantation folks at all. Plantation kings sent someone or went to Africa themselves to get real people who were *not* slaves and make them slaves.

Still, I warn that no curse can alight without a cause. As the Hebrews who were worshipping idols and were warned and warned, but they didn't obey God, so they were taken into captivity and made slaves. Is that also what happened to these people from the continent of Africa? Because no curse can alight without a cause.

The Plantation is a type of HELL, where the Plantation masters and overseers are doing the job of the tormentors in the lower regions of Hades.

Perhaps it was torment that was due because of all the idolatry. I don't question God; I wonder about man's motives and actions in all of this HELL.

We all can do better.

Were those sold into slavery in trouble with God? Were they under judgment with God? Is this why this was all *allowed*? A captive life reflects a captive soul. A soul becomes captive when there's sin. On the other side of the world and in another time the Hebrews went into slavery for **idolatry.** *Is this a carbon copy of that?*

Or did Plantation America cross spiritual lines with God and put *themselves* under judgment with the Lord God? God is long-suffering, but--, are they still under judgment? The curse you send to another will find you; the pit you dig for another, you will fall into it (Bible). God knows the answers to all these questions.

Remember, the Colonists belonged to England and were part of this time captives of England, in a sense, by taxation. **So captive people captured and further imprisoned** *other* **people. This proves that there are levels to HELL.**

While in Plantation America were African slaves required to renounce their *gods*? Yes. That's a common war tactic. The enslaved were not allowed to serve whatever little g *gods* they may have been serving, at least not openly. I really think they were in trouble for idolatry. Like the Hebrews that were taken into captivity they may have been worshipping idol *gods*, and they may have been warned by our Father God to stop. The punishment matches the Hebrews in Egypt, eerily.

Were they warned but they didn't stop?

Now, because of Plantation America all manner of things have happened. And all kinds of things have gotten into these people, into these enslaved people. It's *in them* now.

I'm now chastising the people who have the nerve to ask, *Why are they like that?*

Before you say or think that you're on the *other side* and you got over, you didn't. Remember whatever gets into a person stays there unless it is resisted or driven out by force. Africans brought their pagan *gods* from Africa with them. They were forbidden to worship them--openly. Africans were captured probably for being disobedient and rebellious toward God, they weren't stupid, so they exchanged the names of their pagan *gods* for Catholic saints so they could keep calling on their little g *gods*. And that is who Catholics are worshipping to this day, **pagan African *gods*.**

We don't need anyone calling for the Angels of Africa to this country, they are already here. When Colonists and slave traders captured Africans for slavery, they captured EVERYTHING that was already in that African person, everything in their spirits and souls and brought all of that over here to Plantation America.

If you were born into or thrown onto a slave plantation, you'd certainly be in survival mode, and you might call on any body and anything that you may think could save you. More irony, plantation owners took their slaves to church to get the slaves to serve the *same* God that the Colonists **weren't** serving, because if they were, they wouldn't have had slaves.

# Survival

But still the descendants of these plantations ask, *Why are they like that?*

Well, why do you think they are like that?

If you treat a person like an animal and you put them in barely survivable conditions. Why would you wonder that they are in survival mode? *Are you kidding?*

Survival mode puts people into a fight or flight condition. A lot of stress hormones are released in the body. During times of crisis, chaos, and trauma people enter into **survival mode**. Their normal thinking brain kind of retreats. The brain that thinks and makes critical decisions during stress gets hijacked by the emotions. Multiple hormones are released into the bloodstream. The rational mind becomes less functional or prominent in decision making. The emotional mind mutinies and takes over. This happens to <u>every</u> human and even slaves because slaves were also human, fully human.

So being stuck in survival mode leads to mental and body fatigue. People are upset, angry, on edge, and lashing out. All kinds of bad things happen to them INTERNALLY as well as in their environment. They don't use their brain like they used to. They lose sleep; they may get high blood pressure or other diseases. They're fearing for their life and their safety, *daily*. The brain can't concentrate, there may be memory loss. Due to stomach issues there's improper digestion of food.

A slave may suffer malnutrition for more reasons than stress. Their food is low *on the hog*, it's bad food, leftover crap. Plantation America. These environmental conditions and poor diets left the captives with blood pressure issues, heart disease, heart failure, heart attack, stroke and suppressed immune systems. Hope deferred makes the heart sick. So this person is supposed to go to fields and work? This is demonic.

Therefore, no one should ever ask, *Why are* ***they*** *like that?* They are like that because look at their ancestors, what got into their ancestors got into their bloodline.

If you're **not** in survival mode and your thinking brain isn't hijacked, then you can answer it yourself. *Why do you think they're* ***like*** *that?*

Treat anyone the way that slaves are treated, even your own children, you'll see how they turn out. If you only treat one generation this way, and the effect of that mistreatment *gets in there*, watch and see how their children turn out, because if it **gets in there**, it gets into the bloodline, it gets into the generations. Your grandchildren and onward might be a hot mess.

All these stressors would be happening daily to a slave while they had to work under the threat of beatings or worse.

You couldn't do it. You call out from work if you get a hangnail. No heart.

You who are judging, maybe you should ask yourself why **<u>YOU</u>** are *like that*?

# A Whole Person

A slave is a whole person, not 3/5 of a person. Saying that a whole person is 3/5 of a person does not make it true. You cannot believe that you can just say something different over God's creation, over a human being, enslave and brutalize them, and then call them less than human when you're the person who's behaving--, *oddly*.

That's an attempt to slap God in the face, saying that His creation is not human. That would be blasphemy because God doesn't make junk and He doesn't make partial stuff. I warn you that God's arm is not too short. God's arm is still not too short.

Finally, when slavery is over-- on paper, a recently freed man may think, *Oh good, I'm finally out of this. Now I get to be king.* Yet the oppressor continues to oppress him, hoping he will *never* rise out of survival mode. Hoping he'll never rise to know his own identity, his purpose, and his truth.

Whether this freed man ever gets to reach the level of *king* or just remains a regular free person who is chronically and systematically oppressed into survival mode that's between him and his God. If he is serving Jehovah, the Only Living God, he can overcome.

Serving any other *god*? Forget about it. His captivity will probably get even worse.

This freedman may be so oppressed or so uninspired that he may think of the good of slavery and want to go back to it instead of stepping up and stepping forward. His forward steps may be consistently blocked. Forward may not even seem to be an option, so he may desire to go back to the melons, garlic, cucumbers, and all that *stuff—for free*. If he lets flesh memories and flesh pleasures draw him, he will be pulled backward and into his past. Where *free* meant all of his freedom, time and all the money he would have made and kept for himself in a lifetime, if he worked that hard and was **NOT** a slave.

Has this man been berated, whipped, beaten, defeated enough to go *back* into slavery? That's what the oppressor is probably hoping. Has his spirit been broken down that much, or broken completely? Has despair and desperation gotten into his soul and what is left of it now? What's left of his spirit and of his family if he even has a family anymore?

God is watching, and He may not be at the distance that we think He is. God is closer than we may think.

For those who are free or believe they are free and have broken *out of* survival mode in spite of all opposition, I admonish you, do not desire the king's delicacies. Just because it's what you've seen doesn't make it right. Retaliation and revenge is not what's right. Vengeance is the Lord's, and you cannot fashion yourself to behave like the evil plantation master that was over you.

Do not desire the king's dainties (Proverbs 23:3), because the *king's* things might be your undoing. It may very well be his, also. Don't desire the king's food, not his ice cream, not his liquor, not his money, not the king's drugs, not the king's power, not the king's sin. Especially don't desire the king's women.

Why would you need to do that anyway?

Because your women are too easy, having historically been just *provided* for you? Because they historically have had to work hard just like you, so they haven't had a chance to get dolled up, prettied up, perfumed up and become ladies of leisure?

You want the leisurely type that has leisure because your woman did all their blessed work so they could go to the blessed spa and get their hair and nails done?

*Are you kidding me right now?*

Just as you were stuck on a plantation, working from sunup to sundown, perhaps double shifts or more **with no pay** to enrich the Plantation owner. Ain't nobody in their right mind lusting after Massa just because he's got money. Enslaved man, Freedman, it's *your* money, we all know it's your money--, it's *our* money.

Similarly, the king's women have taken all the hair, facials, and mani-pedi appointments. We can't even get one for those services even if we could afford it—the man formerly known as Massa has our money!

Additionally, why was the plantation master creeping to the slave women if what he had was so satisfying? Fornication and adultery were still sins in Plantation America. God didn't declare open season on anything just because Colonists wanted it that way.

In modern times I admonish you to love your own wife, drink water from your own cistern. Love your women. Be all the man you should be so that your woman can be as feminine as she can be. A woman can only be as feminine as you allow her to be, and that with trust, faith, support, cooperation, and love.

If nothing has changed since that paper of freedom got signed, what's in the average man is cultural and historical *expectancy*. It's not faith in what you **know a proper** relationship could be with your own woman. If you let her *be* a woman, just <u>be</u> a woman and not have to do the work of a man, and also doing everything on her own you'd get a spectacular beauty. Why don't you take some or all of the unnatural burdens off your *own* woman?

You want to help the woman of leisure to remain at leisure because she *looks* better? Well, she's at leisure with nothing but time to primp; this should not be a mystery to anyone. There's no love in that. Not even self-love. That's straight up Plantation Mentality. Until deliverance, if whatever prances in front of your eyes can steal you away. You need deliverance.

In modern day, whatever is showcased on TV for your viewing pleasure is not an option. Do you think God is running TV programming? The *god* of this world is running it. The prince of the powers of the air is running the airwaves unless prayer warriors have pulled down his authority in certain regions and areas. So, what you see on TV is most likely demonic and should be used as teachable moments, not *options* for dating and marriage.

The devil knows that the eyes of a man are never full. Lust of the eye, lust of the flesh, pride of life. Just because it's what you see all the time should not make it what you want. Well, if you have no willpower because your soul has been beat down so much it's weak that could explain a lot. Just because you *see* a thing, such as food, alcohol, cigarettes, women--, just because you see it, you don't have to *want* it.

# Keep It

We all want to make it in life. We all want to be accepted. Your money will make room for you. But when you die in modern times, will you leave all the money you've earned in this life to your former oppressors? You know, the ones that caused all the jacked-up ways that you feel and think and all the jacked-up spiritual stuff that's going on in your life? Are you daft?

I'm talking about Plantation Mentality that was engrained in slaves. You (your ancestors) learned to work for **nothing** in Plantation America. Is that *still in there*? Do you need deliverance from that? Without deliverance, you may perpetuate that behavior, giving all of your life's work, your life's earnings all back to the oppressors.

No! Set your house in order.

All those things that helped your ancestors cope, but they *enjoyed*, can you see now how that was all enticement for control? More of the king's delicacies. Does that still control you? You need deliverance. That keeps your mind in the Wilderness, that keeps your mind on Plantation life that keeps you the same person that you were when you were slave, a slave to the world, perhaps fostered by when your ancestor was a slave on the plantation.

At that time, all the women of color were sweating in the sun, but the Massa's wife pranced by all gussied up, smelling good. Your great, great, great grandpa lusted after that and *lust* got in there, in your bloodline.

What do you think you're doing right now? You didn't invent this; you didn't come up with this idea on your own. Lust did. And it looks like you're working to fulfill a demonic lust mandate into the 3rd and 4th generation of your bloodline. Resist: don't do it.

# DNA

Folks who are worried about vaccines are worried about their DNA changing from receiving vaccines--, which **cannot** happen. Yet, these are the same souls who are willfully allowing the *expression* of their own DNA, to be changed by **not getting deliverance, and continuing to sin and allowing any wicked thing** into their lives.

That's how these changes get *in there.* By the third generation the **expression** of the bloodline DNA is *different* than what it was before there was chronic and unrepented for sin.

When something has changed your soul, when it's changed your spirit, when it's changed your DNA. Let me say more like the way your DNA expresses itself, because experts have found that depression, for example, can affect the way that your DNA expresses itself.

Have you ever considered that in Plantation America a slave, any slave, maybe *all* slaves, could be depressed, and at the very least in despair?

What you do in captivity stays in captivity. No, it doesn't. If it gets *in* you, if it becomes part of you; it goes everywhere you go, it changes you and even your DNA expression. It changes your family life, your household, eventually your bloodline. When it's been in there for three or more generations, it's a stronghold. ***It's in there.***

The slave master, in all his hubris, exalted himself to--, I don't know, *God,* or thinking he's above God, misinterpreting, even deleting parts of the Bible to control other human beings--, especially when you say you come here for religious freedom. This is rich.

I had to write this so I can read it over and again: People who felt oppressed came to the Colonies to settle, *they say* they wanted **religious freedom** and then ultimately, they want freedom from taxation, so then they could then take away the **freedom** --, the entire freedom and the lives of millions of other people--, People Groups of color and tax them at 100%, taking everything from them, and that's rich.

There is nobody I know that I could pay to help me understand that, because it makes absolutely no sense, and it never will make any sense. It is a lie.

It's a lie from the pit of hell. But when you're set free, for real, and you meet God for real, and you start serving God for real, instead of mortal or dead idols you would never act that way. If you were an enslaved person on a plantation, you would be set free indeed, and all strongholds would be broken, all the chains that held you would be broken both in the natural, and in the spirit, and all the chains binding your soul.

Everything holding a man down is broken.

Now you're free. What a glorious day when the soul is free and no longer a Plantation Soul.

# Pick Your Side

Pick your side. We're at the pick your side part of this book.

Still picking sides?

Do you prefer fair-complected people? Colorism. It's all part of the divide and conquer game. Whether you're light- or dark-complected is the basis for colorism.

Pick your side.

Are you hair-struck? What texture of hair you have has gotten so old. It's from Plantation America where the more like Massa you appear to be, the more you're accepted, maybe. WHY is that STILL in there? It's all flesh. It's all from the devil, so stop it. Drop it.

Maybe you're paying people less because of the color of their skin, or because of their ethnic background?

Pick your side.

Regarding working for cheap, for free, know your value. Research to know what your job is worth and ask for what you know you deserve and earn that. And keep it. Keep it for yourself, for your family. Working for free or nearly free, working for less than what others get, even now, is the residual of that. Working for less than what the job actually pays? Know your worth. Ask for what you're worth.

Pick your side.

You're not better than other races. Do not hate other people groups.

Pick your side.

You're not less than other races. Do not hate your own kind.

Pick your side. You're not an animal.

Pick your side. You have no right to treat anyone like an animal, although some people treat their animals better than they treat people.

Pick your side. People cannot be mated and trafficked for money. People belong to God. Hands off.

Pick your side.

Babies cannot be sold. People cannot be sold. Babies are people--, God's creations, His property, not yours. Hands off.

Pick your side.

Men: You are not made for stud service. Get married. Take care of your own kids. Build your own family. Prosper your own bloodline. Build a family legacy.

Pick your side. You cannot own people.

Pick your side. You cannot be owned. You belong to God. You are fearfully and wonderfully made. You cannot be owned. Stay prayed up because everyone--, especially evil people didn't get this memo, and they don't yet know this.

If you think God made someone or a whole group of people less than others, you're probably the less than one for thinking that way.

Pick your side.

# ONE SOUL

# One Soul

Wake up; I've admonished you, wake up. Because the fight is internal, the fight for your soul is *in* you <u>first</u>. The fight is spiritual, and you are spirit. You have a soul, and you live in a body. The fight is *for* your soul.

Plantation America is where a slave was considered 3/5 of a person. The lie that someone is 3/5 of a person is just not true in any way just because someone said it. Further, I wonder if that was the desired outcome of the devil-- if he had hoped to reduce the souls of slaves by 2/5 to make them ineffective in the Earth because they didn't have a **whole soul.**

Wake up, wake up.

The fight is not to assimilate and to make folk who are not like you celebrate you. The fight is that you love God with your *whole soul*. God will MAKE your enemies to be at peace with you. So, the first fight is you fighting for yourself, for your identity, for your identity in Christ. Then you fight to make your soul *whole.*

Beloved, and I pray above all things, that you prosper and be in health even as your soul prospers. (3 John 2)

Fight for your soul to be whole even against daily assaults that come as a result of being in this world. Your soul can't be tied to others or split up and broken up and all over Timbuktu and who knows where. Regarding identity: who does <u>God</u> say that you are? You must know this. You have to know your identity. Your spiritual identity IS your identity.

Secondly, now walk in it. It means every day you have to remind yourself of who you are in Christ, because *nothing* is not happening, something is happening all day. Who are you in Christ? What's your status in Christ? There's no turning back and there's no turning aside.

Thirdly, you need to *speak* who you are, to yourself, to your mirror if you have to, to your family, to your friends, to anyone who will listen to you. If no one will listen, you might have to tell it to the devil, because he needs to know that **you know** who you are and that you walk in authority.

Speak it. Speak the authority that you walk in, in Christ. **You are the boss of evil**, the enemy will try to tell you, *"You're not the boss of me."* But you are the boss of evil, if you are saved and in Christ. It is why God put you here.

I desire to do your will. My God.

Your law is within my heart.

Psalm 40:8

# The Boss

The revelation the Lord shared with me for this message is from Deuteronomy 32:30, that if one can put 1000 to flight, then two can put 10,000 to flight. Here, we're speaking of humans sending angels out to do the will of the Word of God.

Know that there's a counterfeit where the devil will try the opposite. When you say negative things, evil angels (demons) will try to make those negative things you spoke happen *to* you.

If you don't want a defeated life and to have unnecessary battles and wars in life, then guard your mouth and guard your ears so you don't bring trouble on yourself.

But how should one chase a thousand, and two put ten thousand to flight except their rock had sold them and the Lord had shut them up? Deuteronomy 32:30

One soul, one soul-- one **whole** soul. If you don't have your *whole soul*, no wonder your prayers are ineffective. If you're not even able to put the 1000 angels to flight because your soul is not whole, because of sin, because of curses, generational curses, word curses, witchcraft, foolishness, then what do you expect to accomplish in the spirit? In the Earth? How can you be the *boss* of anything or anyone?

You need your whole soul. One whole soul. God deals with us by our spirit and not just by our emotions, not just our will and our intellect, but we have to all line up as a whole soul to put those angels to flight. Our whole soul means our will, emotions, and intellect, well-ordered and put together. Perhaps the diminished soul means diminished authority. **Or maybe it means no authority at all.**

The devil might be saying, *"You ain't the boss of me."* But you are, well you're supposed to be. As long as you are in authority and speaking the voice of the Word of the Lord, when you pray, say, declare and decree, then you are.

The devil doesn't want you to know that you are. You are the boss of him, as long as you walk in your authority. The devil's tactics are to try to make you lose your authority or never know that you have authority--, or both. So instead of standing in faith in your own authority he tries to get you to back down, fall back, or beg someone else to do it for you.

I remember when I was a baby Christian, I watched who I considered to be the big preachers, the important ones, the real Christian-y ones on TV. I would think, *"Look at my life! If I could just get him or him or her to pray for me then I would have it made."*

Over a short time, thank God, I realized that the Bible says that we need to know God for ourselves. At that moment I decided that I'll have to pray for myself. Then I decided I'm going to pray for myself. And that's how this journey started from there to here. So far.

One soul. Do it yourself with your **one soul**. Later when you can join with others do it. But start with yourself.

What is the value of a whole soul? I'd say everything. I say the value of a whole soul is everything because it shows God that you heard Him. It shows God that you listened and that you obeyed and that you have faith. It shows God that you are using your willpower to resist sin so you can stay **whole**. It is showing God that you are prospering your soul, which is what He told you to do. It shows God that you honor Him and that you trust Him, and you love Him. One whole soul. The value of it is priceless because it is priceless to God.

God gave you a whole soul, not a partial soul. God wouldn't give you junk. He wouldn't give you a piece of something. He wouldn't give you a *hooptie*.

The things done in Plantation America blatantly attacked souls and when successful made them into Plantation Souls. Were the things done to slaves in Plantation America enough to break their spirit? Seems that was the goal. Were the things done on the Plantations enough to break one's spirit, were they enough to assault one's soul? Yes, I say, Yes.

Did the devil tell us his intentions when he said that slaves were 3/5 human? Was that the evil formula? Was that the intention to damage the slave's soul down to 3/5? That is splitting the soul, tying at least 2/5 of the soul up in sin, distraction, soul-ties, survival mode, and foolishness.

I don't know how to measure this because the intellect, the emotions, and the will--, that's three parts. If you break down the emotions, you still have 2/3. If you break down the intellect, you still have 2/3. If you break down the will, you still have 2/3. I don't know if there's a weighted value on the emotions, the will and the intellect. Maybe the will is worth more. Perhaps the devil slipped up and gave us a formula that he may not have meant to give us. Maybe the emotions are worth one, the intellect is worth one, and the will is worth 3. That could be why the WILL of slaves is attacked heinously, devastated, and broken. We've got to ask God.

Maybe if you could just knock down the emotions by putting the slaves in survival mode, or if you could knock down the intellect by *keeping* them in survival mode so the cognitive functions of their brains didn't work like it used to, maybe that would knock it down to 3/5. Or, maybe those plantation folks didn't know how to do FRACTIONS?? This is all something to think about. Meditate on, pray about, do research on.

I think it may have been his formula; the devil tells on himself. Did the devil tell his intention when he said that slaves were 3/5 human? I do not believe that plantation owners weren't listening to the devil. They came up with these evil strategies on their *own*? The fact that they were harboring, using, beating, and killing slaves makes them different from evil Egyptian Pharoah's...... *how*?

These tactics, how to be this evil to people and how to beat, rape, and murder them was programmed from hell. Every attack, murder and bloodshed was a sacrifice to whatever evil blood-thirsty *gods* the Colonists served for money, wealth, riches. Sacrifices, they say, is why so many millions didn't even make it through the Middle Passage.

I don't believe they came up with all of this on their own although it was in the wheelhouse of a man's sin nature, their base nature. They called themselves living in civilization, but this is what they did? They had to have some evil spiritual suggestions to tell him how to do this and a *demonic charge* to keep them doing it.

There were some slave owners who didn't want to beat their slaves, so there were whipping stations in town where a slave owner could take his slaves and pay a small fee and have someone there terrorize the slave to try to bring them under submission to the flesh of the plantation owner. Organized evil; this is abhorrent.

The devil loves trauma. He uses it to open doors to either fragment a soul, to capture it or a part of it, and/or slip in some evil demons. Was it the devil's intention to damage the slaves' souls in order to split that soul or diminish it so much that they would lose **authority in the spirit so IF they decided to serve God they'd be at a deficit or a loss**? Has that been his strategy all along? Since Adam & Eve?

These are powerful questions.

If a person's intellect is not empowered and they don't know the Word of God, if they have not studied to show themselves approved, they can end up making unwise or ignorant choices. In a man's decisions he can either build up or compromise and destroy his body and his life.

You need your whole soul, locked and loaded to fight the devil.

# Love Yourself

You are to love yourself. The self that God made you to be, not the *version* of yourself that your captor has convinced you that you are, to control you. That same captor that was working either for God or for not-God. Which one do you think would brutalize you like that, threatening beatings, murder, amputations, in Plantation America? I would say, not-God.

Once free, on paper, the most important part of your fight is internal. Fight to change what happened *to* you and your bloodline in Plantation America. Fight for deliverance, for restoration, to be reset to what and who God intended you to be.

What happened to you? What happened in the first place that allowed the curse? Because the curse causeless will not alight. I remind you that God kept telling the Hebrews if they kept worshipping idols that He would send them into captivity and into captivity, in Egypt they went for 430 years. I wonder sometimes if God had them in captivity for the same number of years that they were worshipping the idols when they were ignoring God's warnings.

It's as though God said, *If you want to worship false gods, there's Egypt, a land of false **gods**, have at it.*

Later, the Africans may have been under God's judgment and God's hand of protection was not as close as it had been. Did somebody try to lift them up and redeem them or did they get used, abused and further cursed? Talk about kicking a man when he's down.

See, that's the devil for you, his trick is for you to be under judgment from God for the very thing that the devil tempted or tricked you into doing in the first place. Now you're out of authority, you're out of place, you're out of position. You know the devil's really gonna sock it to you, because right now you're weak which is when you really need to be the boss of him. But you're not.

Now that there's freedom, ***on paper***, you need to ask yourself, is there freedom in the Spirit or are there still curses in force against me? If so, am I perpetuating the evil by agreeing with the curse(s)? And if you're agreeing with it, are you doing it on purpose or are you doing it in ignorance?

God sets a man free, but that man must, by submitting to the Holy Spirit, do some soul work to prosper his soul on his own.

What is your reason for being other than to be yourself? Your reason for being is not to remain captive. Your reason for being is not to remain a people pleaser; it's not to keep stepping and to keep fetching.

The Emancipation Proclamation is signed, making you instantly free on paper, but what has 250 years of *what happened* done to you down your family line? What has 250 years of all of those things that have happened done to you, to your mind, to your will, to your intellect, to your soul? All those *somethings*, such as sexual sin because they created soul ties which further depletes your soul, they diminish the wholeness of your soul, which diminishes your authority in the Earth and in the Spirit.

The only sex that is legal is that with your legally married spouse. So let me drop this on you: For all we know *spirit spouse* could have come down your generations from forced, fornication, adultery, sex on the Plantation.

# Do The Work

In interpersonal matters they say it takes a month for every year to get over a broken relationship, then 250 years of captivity should have taken about 25 months to get the captivity, the survival mindset, and soul damage out.

But that's only if some work was being done toward that.

I suspect that very few, if any, were doing any work to get over it, because humans are creatures of habit and flesh can be lazy. Some are longing for the good old days of slavery instead of using faith to move into the Promised Land.

They're just going around the same old trail over and over, using *expectancy* instead of faith, expecting the same old results and getting the same old results or worse.

The captor doesn't want to stop being the captor, the oppressor and the master. It's very convenient for him. What work would he do to be better than he was during Plantation America times? He already thought he was the greatest. Everything that is your fault, you may not see or realize it as a problem.

The captive--, come on, we can look at the residual effects of how things got into enslaved peoples' bloodlines to see that more work needs to be done, starting with prayer, resisting the devil, deliverance, salvation--, everything. Not necessarily in that order, but still all of that. Everything that is your problem may not be your fault.

It was hanging on to the captivity practices and mindsets that made for the 40 years of Wilderness for the Israelites. Those people had Egypt *in* them, and God wasn't even letting them get into the Promised Land until Moses struck a substitution deal with God. Moses didn't go in, so the rest could go in, which is the type and shadow of Jesus our Christ.

People are still hanging on to Plantation Mentality, Plantation mindsets, I'm not even talking about, the hundred-plus years of Jim Crow and even up to now that's causing all kinds of spiritual and natural issues.

Yeah, but the Emancipation Proclamation has been signed, you say. Yeah, forcibly. It's a signed document in the natural; it doesn't make anybody free, not really--, just on paper. It also doesn't make the captor, the oppressor any different either. So, if you're waiting for the guy who oppressed you to start liking you and to stop oppressing you, you had better start accepting yourself. You'd better break out of survival mindset and think, make critical decisions for **yourself** and your life.

Get in the Word, get in the presence of God. Get deliverance, spiritual work is soul work. Settle down out of survival mode, I bet you will like yourself then. I bet you will love yourself.

You'd better start becoming yourself right now. There's nothing else to wait for. There's no reason to wait. Oh, do we need God? Yes, we do.

# The Blood Is Crying Out

If you were the aggressor or the oppressor in your bloodline, you need to repent, and renounce for yourself and for the sake of your bloodline. The blood of millions cries out from the ground on this land, on *this* soil. I'm not even talking about the Middle Passage, the millions of lives lost there, like blood offerings to the evil water kingdom in exchange for passage through the cold, cold Atlantic, in exchange for passage for themselves as they lusted for wealth and riches.

The blood is still crying out even when the people think that the secrets that they've buried in the soil are hidden; **the blood is crying** out from the ground. You may think it's buried, but it can't be hidden. It will come to light.

All those people who were lost, God knows their names. God sees them. Even if you think other people don't know what you or your people did, God knows. God can hear the voice of the millions killed or sacrificed demonically for the lust of money. Yeah, plantation money.

Even now, God is asking, *Where's your brother?*

Because Cain hated Abel. Yeah, but Cain wanted *stuff.* He wanted to keep the stuff that God told him to steward over and to bring part of it to God. Cain hated Abel because Abel obeyed God. If Cain and Abel had been in Vegas, Abel would have told what happened in Vegas, while Cain would have continued to try to hide it, but Cain's secret told on him.

In Plantation America, plantation owners wanted all the *stuff.* They thought that what they did to accomplish that, what they did on the Plantation is hidden but it's not. All the dead, beaten, murdered, lynched, burnt, drowned and sacrificed *Abel's* are still crying out from the ground.

Every lie that is spoken over you to dominate you, to manipulate you, to control you, is still a lie and it is still a curse. If you've been cursed by the words that you've heard, or the things that you have been forced to hear, or the things that you've allowed *in* just to cope, or the things that you thought were okay because you didn't have the education or the knowledge of the truth to know how to fight it or know how to resist it, you need deliverance.

When I say, forced to hear I am speaking of bloodline curses that originated in Plantation America that granny and great granny, even your parents still believe, speak—repeating the words of their captors over their own children, and then walking it out. I'm talking about remnants of evil plantation curses whether people realized it or not – those curses **got in there.** Cursed mindsets such as, *"Sonny, don't try to make too much of yourself if you don't want to make enemies. Just do enough to get along."*

If you've been cursed by the words that you yourself have repeated, that you've spoken over yourself or your family in anger, haste, frustration or ignorance, repent now. Never repeat what the enemy says to you, and about you, not in your mind and definitely **never out loud.**

Do not perpetuate the curse that you've been indoctrinated to believe by speaking it. Ever.

Have you ever taken the time to separate out what you know to be true, what you believe to be true from being on remote and just repeating the stuff you've heard your parents and grandparents repeat? Can you? If you can't you need deliverance. If you can, praise God; be set free!

Wake up! The fight is internal **first**, and mostly the fight is *in* you. The fight is *spiritual,* and you are spirit. You have a soul and you are living in a body. The fight is for your soul.

The fight is not to assimilate, to make folk like you, especially folk who are not like you. The fight is that you love God with your whole soul. The first fight is you fighting for yourself, for your identity in Christ. Plantation America stole more identities than any of us may have ever imagined. You must fight for your identity and your whole soul. Your soul can't be split up. Don't let it get split up. It can't be all over town and all over who knows where.

# Do You Hear the Blood?

Oh, there's so much blood polluting the Earth and screaming out from the ground on this soil, on this land, and on a lot of other lands too. Only God can help us and forgive us and set us back on right course. We turn from our wicked ways and turn to Him and seek His face. He can help us, He can deliver us, He can bring us out and bring evil out of us.

But we must submit to the Holy Spirit and do our own soul work in our families, in ourselves, and in our bloodline, instead of just carrying on business as usual.

Acceptance from the previous oppressor, or current oppressor is not the same as acceptance from God, because they are not God. If they were God, they would have been behaving in a godly manner. There would have been no slaves and no resultant curses from operation Plantation America.

Instead of letting things wax on bolder in your bloodline and in your household, do some soul work and get rid of those oppressions that have beset your bloodline so you can be a whole soul again and walk in your God-given authority and spiritual power.

Sin is sin. God did not suspend spiritual laws for the 250 years of Plantation America. Even if no one died, and we know millions did, blood that cries out is the blood of murders, beatings, lynchings, sex sins, anywhere seed or DNA was spilled or exchanged. That was the FIRE of sin, and the smell of smoke is still on anyone or anyone whose family was involved in Plantation America.

We should all be aware that more blood than that of Plantation America was spilled on this soil and if we think God is winking at that, think again.

The Document was signed, and we moved on? Just because we think we turned a deaf ear on the blood that is still crying out doesn't mean that God doesn't hear it. It doesn't mean that those with ears to hear don't hear those cries.

This land needs healing and repentance; we all need God.

# Do We Heal?

Coming out of captivity the first thing to consider is healing and restoration. Do we wander or do we heal? Do we do the work and heal?

After the Emancipation Proclamation was a wilderness period for America. What did we do in that? Did we choose to or try to heal?

It just struck me that folks in the same bloodline, should gather together, because God said to do it. He said don't forsake to gather together, I'll add, not just in church, but related people--, family should get together regularly. Yeah, to socialize and have fun, but also to help one another. Not just to help each other pay bills keeping those family and generational money altars hot. We shouldn't gather just to find out the latest fashion and the latest dances, or to reminisce over the good old days, or lost loved ones, but to help the entire family to heal in their souls and also to avoid spiritual traps of the enemy.

We should gather to lift one another up and pray.

If one puts 1000 to flight and two 10,000, I've often wondered does three put 100,000 of flight, 4, a million? I don't know, I've just wondered that.

Two putting 10,000 Angels to flight, is when two are **agreeing**. Are two who *say* they are agreeing *really* agreeing? Are the two that agree, are they both two *whole* souls? Are you working with the whole soul? And is the person who's agreeing with you, are they also working with a *whole* soul? You better know.

Can you imagine God looking over into that family gathering and saying, ***"Look at them laughing and eating and drinking and dancing because you know, a paper was signed and they're free. Look at all that power in that room, and they're doing nothing with it. Yeah, they'll call Me tomorrow, to ask Me to save them from something or other. When they have the power right now, right there in that room, to put angels to flight--, Angels that are waiting to do the will of the Word of God.***

*"Why don't they pray? Why don't they decree and declare? Why don't they?*

*"Oh, it's because of the plantation. The plantation mentality. It's still in them. They were forbidden to pray. They had no Bible. They were forbidden to read if they did have a book."*

What about now? Yeah, what about now? See that's the kind of stuff that got into the generations, that created strongholds in captive individuals, families, and in bloodlines.

Running to the captors and the oppressors, living their same harmful lifestyle, desiring the *king's* dainties instead of using your own power and fighting against it is what makes the contract with the captor. All things are spiritual, so it's making that spiritual contract bona fide.

Even if in survival mode, in Plantation America, your ancestor didn't agree to or participate in sin to just survive, he/she just made a deal. That deal was not just for himself or herself it is a **binding contract that implicates the entire bloodline.**

If you sin, when you sin, you do the same. Even if you believe you're saved, and you commit unrepented sin, you've signed up your **family** into the 3$^{rd}$ and 4$^{th}$ generation. If you/your family is not saved, you've signed them up into the 10$^{th}$ to 14$^{th}$ generations. When you give no thought of tomorrow, just today, just survival--, this is what can happen to not just yourself, but your family's bloodline. Your whole family just got signed up for the family plan. But you may think you just signed up for the fun of it for right now. Just for you, and then you're gonna move on.

This isn't Vegas, but even if it were...

You don't move on. You cannot move on because the chains of Plantation America were as real as spiritual chains in the spirit.

Because that thing you did, the thing you participated in, the thing you watched, did or allowed to happen to you, got in you. It changed you. You just signed up your whole family, your household, for generations. **Unless God, unless you see God**, unless you renounce it, repent and turn away from it. And receive deliverance from he demons that are already enforcing the curse(s).

Even if the sin was FORCED on you; it is still sin and all that spiritual contractual fallout is legal. Women especially, consider who you marry, a sinful bad boy can sign you up for all kinds of covenants and curses that you know nothing about. And there you'll be wondering, *What has happened to my life? Why don't I have the favor of God anymore?*

Eve signed Adam up.

We all need salvation and deliverance.

Until someone in your family line, someone in authority, someone with a whole soul in your family line renounces, cancels, and breaks this contract (covenant) your family may be stuck. It won't be until somebody in your bloodline stands in the gap and gets deliverance from this curse (these curses). And the rest of the family follows suit. You all need to resist the devil, get delivered and develop the Fruit of the Spirit and do not do any of the works of the flesh.

Don't let the soul types of Plantation America still be running and ruining your life.

# Benediction

This has been Black History Month. This is the part, this is the month, this is the book intended to remind you of who you are, who you used to be. Who you're supposed to be and how to get back to all that. And the key is Jesus, and the key is a whole soul.

Shalom.

For comprehensive prayers: **Breaking the Curses of Slavery: Prayers for African Americans** by Pamela Burgess Main.

And/or: **The Angela Project Presents 40 Days of Prayer**: for the Liberation of American Descendants of Slavery by Cheri Mills.

# Other books by this author

AK: The Adventures of the Agape Kid

Already Married in the Spirit: *Why You May Not Be Maied in the Natural*

AMONG SOME THIEVES

Ancestral Powers

Anti-Marriage, *The Spirit of*

Backstabbers https://a.co/d/gi8iBxf

Barrenness, *Prayers Against* https://a.co/d/feUltIs

Battlefield of Marriage, *The*

Beauty Curses, *Warfare Prayers Against* https://a.co/d/5Xlc2OM

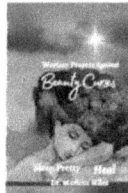

Beware of the Dog: Prayers Against Dogs in the Dream.

Bless Your Food: *Let the Dining Table be Undefiled*

Blindsided: *Has the Old Man Bewitched You?* https://a.co/d/5O2fLLR

Break Free from Collective Captivity

Broken Spirits & Dry Bones

Casting Down Imaginations

Churchzilla, The Wanna-Be, Supposed-to-be Bride of Christ

Courts of Marriage: Prayers for Marriage in the Courts of Heaven *(prayerbook)* https://a.co/d/cNAdgAq

Courtroom Warfare @ Midnight *(prayerbook)* https://a.co/d/5fc7Qdp

Demonic Cobwebs *(prayerbook)* https://a.co/d/fp9Oa2H

Every Evil Bird https://a.co/d/hF1kh1O

Gates of Thanksgiving

Demonic Time Bombs

Demons Hate Questions

Devil Loves Trauma, *The*

Devil Weapons: Unforgiveness, Bitterness,…

The Devourers: Thieves of Darkness 2

Do Not Swear by the Moon

Don't Refuse Me, Lord (4 book series)

https://a.co/d/idP34LG

Dream Defilement

The Emptiers: *Thieves of Darkness, 1* https://a.co/d/5I4n5mc

Evil Touch

Failed Assignment

Fantasy Spirit Spouse https://a.co/d/hW7oYbX

FAT Demons (The): *Breaking Demonic Curses*
https://a.co/d/4kP8wV1

The Fold (5-book series)

- The Fold (Book 1)
- Name Your Seed (Book 2)
- The Poor Attitudes of Money (3)
- Do Not Orphan Your Seed (4)
- For the Sake of the Gospel (5)
- My Sowing Journal

Gang Ups: Touch Not God's Anointed

Getting Rid of Evil Spiritual Food

https://a.co/d/i2L3WYQ

got HEALING? Verses for Life

got LOVE? Verses for Life

got HOPE? Verses for Life

got money? https://a.co/d/g2av41N

How to Dental Assist

How to Dental Assist2: Be Productive, Not
Wasteful

How to STOP Being a Blind Witch or Warlock

I Take It Back

Legacy

Let Me Have A Dollar's Wo
https://a.co/d/h8F8XgE

Level the Playing Field

Living for the NOW of God

Lose My Location https://a.co/d/crD6mV9

Love Breaks Your Heart

Made Perfect In Love

Man Safari, *The*

Marriage Ed. Rules of Engagement & Marriage

Made Perfect in Love

Money Hunters: Beware of Those

Money on the Altar https://a.co/d/4EqJ2Nr

Mulberry Tree, *The* https://a.co/d/9nR9rRb

Motherboard (The) ~ *Soul Prosperity Series*

Name Your Seed

Occupy: *Until I Return*

Plantation Souls

Players Gonna Play

Power Money: Nine Times the Tithe
https://a.co/d/gRt41gy

The Power of Wealth *(forthcoming)*

Powers Above

The Robe, Part 1, The Lessons of Joseph

The Robe, Part II, The Lessons of Joseph

Seasons of Grief

Seasons of Waiting

Seasons of War

Second Marriage, Third--, *Any Marriage*

https://a.co/d/6m6GN4N

Sift You Like Wheat

Six Men Short: What Has Happened to all the Men?

Soul Prosperity soul prosperity series 3

https://a.co/d/5p8YvCN

Souls Captivity soul prosperity series 2

The Spirit of Anti-Marriage

Spirits of Death, Hell & the Grave, Pass Over Me and My House

Throne of Grace: Courtroom Prayer

Warfare Prayer Against Poverty
https://a.co/d/bZ611Yu

The Spirit of Poverty

StarStruck

SUNBLOCK

The Swallowers: *Thieves of Darkness,* 3

Take It Back

This Is NOT That: How to Keep Demons from Coming at You

Time Is of the Essence

Too Many Wives: *Why You Have Lady Problems*

Tormenting Spirits   https://a.co/d/dAogEJf

Toxic Souls

Triangular Power *(series)*

- Powers Above
- SUNBLOCK
- Do Not Swear by the Moon
- STARSTRUCK

Unbreak My Heart: *Don't Let Me Die*

Uncontested Doom

Unguarded Hours, *The*

Unseen Life, *The* (forthcoming)

Upgrade: How to Get Out of Survival Mode

- Toxic Souls (Book 2 of series)
- Legacy (Book 3 of series)

The Wasters: *Thieves of Darkness,* Bk 2
https://a.co/d/bUvI9Jo

What Have You to Declare? What Do You Have With You from Where You've Been?

When I Was A Child, *I Prayed As a Child*

When the Devourer is Rebuked

https://a.co/d/1HVv8oq

**The Wilderness Romance** *(series)* This series is about conducting a Godly relationship and marriage with someone who is a Wilderness person. *The Social Wilderness*

- *The Sexual Wilderness*
- *The Spiritual Wilderness*

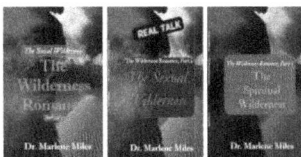

## Other Series

**Spirit Spouse books:** https://a.co/d/9VehDSo

https://a.co/d/97sKOwm

**Battlefield of Marriage, The** https://a.co/d/eUDzizO

**Players Gonna Play** https://a.co/d/2hzGw3N

## Matters of the Heart

Made Perfect in Love https://a.co/d/70MQW3O

Love Breaks Your Heart https://a.co/d/4KvuQLZ

Unbreak My Heart https://a.co/d/84ceZ6M

Broken Spirits & Dry Bones https://a.co/d/e6iedNP

## Thieves of Darkness series

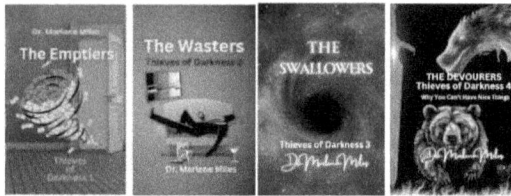

The Emptiers https://a.co/d/heio0dO

The Wasters https://a.co/d/5TG1iNQ

The Swallowers https://a.co/d/1jWhM6G

The Devourers: Why We Can't Have Nice Things
https://a.co/d/87Tejbf

Triangular Powers https://a.co/d/aUCjAWC

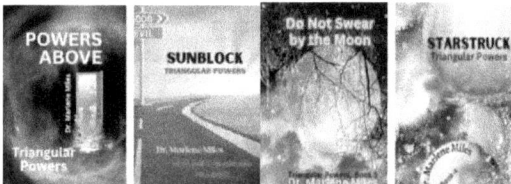

Upgrade (series) *How to Get Out of Survival Mode*
https://a.co/d/aTERhX0

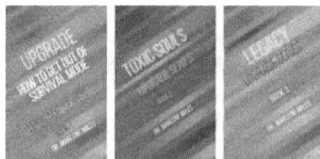

www.ingramcontent.com/pod-product-compliance
Lightning Source LLC
LaVergne TN
LVHW051419080426
835508LV00022B/3166